To Joan -
my soul-kin &
sacred circle guru -
let's dance into the
next chapter!
♡ January.

D0515160

Leaning
Toward
Knowing

Leaning Toward Knowing

January Handl

River Sanctuary
PUBLISHING

Leaning Toward Knowing
Copyright © 2011 by January Handl

All rights reserved. No part of this book may be reproduced, stored in a retrieval system, or transmitted, in any form or by any means, electronic, mechanical, photocopying, recording, or otherwise, without the written prior permission of the author except in the case of brief quotations embodied in critical articles and reviews.

Cover design by Markos-Cory Moreno
Interior design by DreamWriter (Dreamwriterservices.com)

ISBN 978-1-935914-08-2

Printed in the United States of America

RIVER SANCTUARY PUBLISHING
P.O Box 1561
Felton, CA 95018
www.riversanctuarypublishing.com
Dedicated to the spiritual awakening of the New Earth

*To my amazing friends, family,
and colleagues who daily inspire
me...especially to the children.*

The Questions We Live

In which way can we feed each other
The answers to the questions we live?
How do we know when the other is full,
Or when they have plenty to give?

How do we know what sustains us,
During the tempest times of life
How do we know what holds us,
During the storms of emotional strife?

Can we listen to another's hunger,
Can we allow their desires to rise
Can we hear our own heart's thunder,
Can we find center's compromise?

Do we quiet our restless searching
Do we surrender to the pull of tide
Do we walk into the waves unending
With our heart and our arms open wide?

Contents

Revelations while waiting for chamomile tea 1
Innocence and Pain   2
Cory and the Divorce 3
These Children of Others   4
From the Grave   6
Letter To The World 7
Dog Shit Epiphany   8
Middle Age Winter Madness 9
Mother   10
Next Step   12
Truth of Our Dwindling   13
Ode to Our Bed   14
On Bee-ing Flowers   17
On Watching My Dogs Pretend to Be Cows   18
Plums 19
Pop Bill   20
Revising the editor   21
Sophia Grace   22
Soul Kin   23
On This Side   24
Being Hope   25
Fire and Ash   26
Watching Jonah learn to skip 27
Humanity   28
After 20 Minutes of Solo Ecstatic Dancing on my Living Room Floor
29
Glimpsing Miracles   30
Just Now   32
The Edge of Aging   33
Completeness 34
Israel and Palestine   10/15/00   35
Let it Be   36
For my mama on her 67th Birthday   38
About the Author   41

Revelations while waiting for chamomile tea

Rain pours on the oblivious crow
hunting worms on the lawn

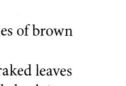

The naked patches of brown
under the tree
show where the raked leaves
no longer crumble back into
sustenance for the living

Suddenly it is obvious this
self-consuming
universe is nothing, nothing
      nothing taking shape and form

The water turns to steam
for my tea
what journey back to One
          is evaporation?

Over and over again
we spin in and out
of existence and
grab onto moments
of consciousness.

we finally evolve to know
of our deaths,
     – and so our lives.

Aware of our minute particle
in the weaving of
what is beyond hope for the mind to grasp –
      the heart leans
         toward knowing.

Innocence and Pain

A young child,
open-faced as a sunflower
turning toward the light,
asked me with an earnest worry
creasing her wonder
as she gently fingered
the earrings dangling from
my ears:
Do those hurt you
very much?

I smiled inside.

I told
her it was only
the initial point of contact,
or separation
and my own fears
that caused acute pain,
which faded daily until
the scarring of the
hole left behind
protected me, allowed me
to decorate myself
leaving only the tender
memory of the moment of
piercing.

I gave a silent blessing
for her piercings
yet to come.

Cory and the Divorce

In the deep black
a tearing of bright white flared,
fell and caught my breath,
as I was thinking of you
as a baby, toddler –
                    young man.

Right now is an impossibly
painful time
and your mommy is like
broken safety glass,
shattered, but held together
by some thin layer of
                    survival.

And in your pain you want to smash her
until the fractures make sense to you;
there is no sense in the ocean of anger in which
you have swam your whole life,
there is no blame,
there is only the charred remains
of the wounded people who
could do no more
                    than is done.

Gentle, please be gentle –
no matter the swing of your hammer
of anguish,
in the end it is you who end up
                    in bitter pieces.

These Children of Others
– for my fellow preschool teachers

My black tank top and blue jeans
heaped in the corner of the bathroom
are covered in spatters
of bright colored paint
from today's messy project

I reach into the pockets so I
don't clog the washer again
with the proudly presented
treasures
of sequins, rocks, flowers
bestowed by the little ones

These children in the here and now,
about to launch into the next phase
of schooling…
From baby to toddler to
these tender, blossoming years
of self-hood, right before
being herded into slaughter-house school
systems that will devour
their natural bends and soft spots,
nibble away their sharp edges,
gnaw at their birthright certainty in self
making every effort to carve them into
one thing
instead of allowing their unique inner curves, cells,
naked knowingness, raw courage
to guide their curiosities toward
truth and wholeness –
THE ONE THING

We love them
these children of others;
we are pulled into the now
by the vibrancy of their being
we become a part of the dance of their
lives, holding, tending, demanding,
guiding, offering illumination, sharing,
letting go…
And we are as schooled by them
                                    as they, us

we carry their lessons, stories and reflections,
in tiny tremors and vibrations,
in our very being- becoming humbled
                          by their giant love

                    and how much we need it.

From the Grave

I am tired of the gravity of this existence –
not the type of solemnity of focus
but the type that holds us fast against the
Spinning Planet
constantly tugging me toward its center
weighting my chest with trivial pursuits
threaded with fear
I can't even just give in and be pinned
with my face in the pungent debris
of the bits of those others
who have finally succumbed to the
pulls and pressures of the inevitable
Spin of Being
because gravity's inertia keeps my
feet plodding forward
toward some unknown
but unavoidable trajectory
where mad paddling, or panicked
thrashing about
only exhausts what momentum was
keeping my now-ness
from flying into past flashes
and future phantoms.

Sometimes
it is all
I can do
to breathe.

Letter To The World

Listen,
The thing is
we come to these amazing machines –these bodies of flesh and birth and death
and rebirth,
From cellular to macro, each part whole unto itself, each part flawed and
wounded and limited
And we strive toward a perfection that can't be
And then we add the feelings that make it all worthwhile, difficult, unbearable,
amazing
And every choice, every circumstance, every interaction keeps leading us to an
inevitable or shifting next step, and there are no easy answers and it is all so
simple, completely hazy in its complexity and starkly obvious in its clarity,
And we project our fears and wonders, our tears and temptations, or dreads and
desires on the all: the other bodies spirits minds around us, the boundaries of
our skin a lie, a lie we asked for, a lie we must live and grow with until the truth
seeps in and strips away the illusions of separateness and the fire of our passions
burns us back to the innocence that continues to remain a stable core despite
what the chattering of the mind that keeps pestering us with distractions tries to
keep us believing – a test of focus, a test of mundane mechanics of life,
a savoring of the miracles that our relativity and connected nature keeps
us from being utterly alone, adrift and away.
Listen,
We are here, now
Give in to that
Be that
I will too.

Dog Shit Epiphany

Hunched in front of the heater,
my back soaking in the radiant heat,
with my hand I feel the outline of my foot-
where I end and everything else
begins.
And I remember my dog shit
epiphany
how looking down at the crumbling
into nothing
piles of my largest complaint as
a dog's partner
I realize
                  Thou art that
And I know I am also
                  God knowing this
48 years old and this small me
Is crumbling underfoot
this big me is amused and sad

Middle Age Winter Madness

Suddenly tired of trying to comfort the
insurance woman on the telephone,
who, upon hearing to
her seemingly innocent
questions about
emergency contacts
And
life and health insurance
And
who drove what auto

my steadily more tearful
answers
ragged, jagged words
...My dad died
I'm not working there
My husband and I are separated
They are totally independent now...

Began to stammer her apologies
For my life
Her voice held genuine regret
For my pain –
She expressed sympathy that made me say

Don't worry spring is coming.

I was in a good mood when I picked up the phone.

Mother

Once a Native American man
told me that if you
lie face down
with head pointed north
and feet pointed south
the earth mother
would accept any grief
in your heart
                    cleansing you, freeing
                                        you

So at a point
when grief was
a tight fist
in my chest
and every sigh
only seemed to deepen
the grasp of sorrow
and force the arrow
of suffering,
further and further
                    into my withering
                                        soul

I lay down with
my face in the summer-dry
redwood duff,
let the fragrance seep past my
nose stuffed with the tears
that dripped from my chin,
                    felt my heart
                                        open

to the silent hum of
the world
while birds and insects
added their
unique voices to a choir
of liquid staccato forest noises;
the ground both received
and rejected
        my bones and body's
            weight

And sure enough,
she opened her womb
accepted seeds of
fear, shame, weariness, sadness
      the pressure eased –
            enough

Guiltily,
I offered an exchange, some
of my sufferings for hers
only suddenly knowing that
her pain was too great for
me to hold;
her suffering was not
understandable
      by the little ones
         she holds.

Next Step

I stand on the brink,
the very crumbling edge,
the launching point,
the point of no return,
where earth, sea and sky
choose sides.
And though my knees tremble
and though my thoughts are
wildly scrambled
I know the next step
is the inevitable culmination
of all past moments.
I breathe in the measured
perfection of anticipation
the long wait/weight is over
as I step
as I leap
into the unknown.

Truth of Our Dwindling

I didn't create this monster
that looms between us,
I just said its name out loud.

I didn't hammer on the foundations
of our love together
I just pointed to the
hairline fracture that
snaked down the middle of it.

I didn't withdraw my interest
in this unknown venture
I just voiced the sensation
of the drifting apart
in the wide ocean of our lives.

When you accuse me of seeking
the end of things as we know it
I have to reflect that
you
have been seeking it in silence
for longer than I knew.

I have to be the one to
open wide the chasm in our hearts
and shout until my throat dries
in guttural sobs that
acknowledge the pain of parting

I am the instrument through which
the truth of our dwindling
tether finds a way to shine

as brightly as we did when
we knew we were for each other.

Ode to Our Bed

That warm-smelling comfort,
with the 420 count sheets
that you say are
    too slippery
        when we fuck

Our bed's summer outfit
just cool sheets with our feet stuck out
not the winter get up of white flannel duvet, no top sheet
easy to make each morning
Traces of patterns of the
salt crusted stains of
our sweat
    and blood
        our tears

Though there seem to be less of those
now that this bed knows
the children are grown and out on their own adventures
Not the past Sunday mornings
in night- warmed blankets
glory-lighted romps with giggling babies between us
and rituals with teddy bears and chants of "do....nuts"!

Yet also witness of angry moments of sobbing
and straight-backed certainty
In my rightness,
my words to myself
ringing full
    of self-pity
        and extremes
allowing the bed to stand for
my indignation and hurt –

My proclamations of withdrawal from the current conflict
and the bleached thinness of the materials of which we are made

Some nights of knotted bed clothes
tortured tosses and turns
vibrations of to-do lists and words uttered
dread of the mornings duties, or excited for the next day's promise
reaching into my sleep
keeping the surface of my awareness
just
          at the
                    eyelids

And those moan-filled moments of love making
an island of focus
surrendering to your fingers and mouth's
sure knowing
          of my
                    tender yearnings,
the gap between our bodies
shrinking to non-existence

Or fierce illuminated memories
crazy changing shadows on the covers
contractions coming every 8 minutes for 2 minutes at a time
for 2 days and nights
and only when you held me
could I doze into the gift of
                    your smell,
                              warmth and skin

But mostly ordinary
                    days,
                              weeks,
                                        years,
this refuge of familiarity in aroma
sighing out the burdens of the day,
welcoming the relief from the body's
weight,
          pains
                    and weakness

Fever-baked and dream-drenched,
our wrinkled pillows
cradling the burbling
over flow
          of our
                    hearts and minds

On Bee-ing Flowers

On Flowers

So blatantly sexual
erect, jutting pistil
stiff stamen, coated with the
other half of the equation
surrounded by the
vulvic vivid
petals that spiral
senses toward the center
of it all
heady aroma provides
drunken ecstatic
loss of mind
finding
Self.

Makes me wanna be a bee.

On Bees

Slow meandering
approach
gentle landing, begins
the dance,
complete focus
of stroke and caress,
lip smacking, tongue probing
tastes of honey dew
nectar
full body coating of the
juices of love making
creation is
sending flying a
satiated, heavy-lidded
creature.

Makes me wanna be a flower.

On Watching My Dogs Pretend to Be Cows

We wandered the land,
our noses munching smells –
grazing on the ghosts of
what has passed,
the sunlight held up our heavy bodies
golden upon our backs.

And grinding on
partially digested ideas
for the third time,
our lowing calls
reminded each other
that we remain connected,
sometimes in that lonely sort
of way.

Our hooves felt the coolness
of the grasses, grainy pathways
over muddy earth,
the heavenly body's burn
turned to food for the masses.

And the slowness of the
present movement
seemed right without thinking.

Plums

At first we all brimmed
with excitement and wistful anticipation
the last two winter's rains had
stolen all but
            a few blossoms.

Now the tree slumped with
the weight of ripening,
and impatience brought
the first taste of sweetness
surrounded with a sour that stopped
            at one bite.

Soon the first bites of "just right"
flesh of sunlight turned manna
reunited us with the earth's
subtle unique configurations
of the same
            bits and pieces.

Then turned into frenzied feasting
picking and offering
fullness and now satiated, now gorged
the ground received the multitudes
of bountiful sloppy, ferment-pungent return
            to the mass source.

And everyone gave up keeping up
the deer, the squirrels and jays and woodpeckers
and me
and the war of clean up
haul and dump
turned to cursing the bounty
            of ambrosial delight –

though today with the sunlight loving my back
and shoulders
and the last soldiers of the last battle scooped
up into
the compost of other lives,
the bees still doing their work,
I am back to admiring
            the flow of the plum.

Pop Bill

In the forbidden car
in my grandparent's driveway,
my brother and I played at freedom.
Too short legs strove toward the power pedal,
driving everywhere we wanted
pulling levers, pushing buttons,
short enough to stand on the seats.
I found Pop Bill's jack knife
in the treasure trove of
the glove compartment.
Fascination with denied danger pulled
past being compliant – the thrill
of going beyond
pushed me even further.
Determination as steeled as the edge
I wanted to wield,
my small fingers found no purchase
to pull open the many instruments.
As always, I relied on my mouth
and without thought pulled
the cold notch with my teeth,   A sudden warm hand, calm
only to have the horror of it snap   pulled into Pop Bill's lap.
in a shock of pain   His adult strength
against my lower lip.   freeing me from my shame,
My brother's wide-eyed look   his gentle rocking slowing my burning tears
falling out of the car, now   my burning face
sure of being caught –   finger under my chin,
left me abandoned,   wiping my face and mouth
watching the drips of blood.   with the man-scented hankie,
                                       stilling my hiccups,
                                       forgiving my youth
                                                 remembering his own.

Revising the editor

Limits, rules, restrictions, guidelines, walls,
trigger my auto-response of
arising fierce Kali-spirit
that demands the shaking off
of the yoke burdening my shoulders,
spitting out the bit between my teeth,
severing the ball and chain cutting into my ankle,
and pulling the barbed wire from around my throat,
to run wildly into
the free dark woods of my intuition

Only to wander
Confused at the confusion that
my primal need for freedom
might cause the rest of the selves around
who earnestly want to understand
what I am trying to convey…
Beyond my defenses that protect where my heart
has been inscribed on the page
Is my yearning to connect deeply
using the instrument of my body/mind/ heart
and yours.
Truth must have some way
to the sacred water
that runs through us all

Slowly back stepping toward
my perceived prison
and now seeing
Walls were intricate bridges
Structure wanted not to contain
but to lend a skin of coherence.
Rules were noble agreements,
lending a lantern
of Illuminated common language,
limits only the background upon
which to create the limitless forms.

Finally

I get it –

the edit.

Sophia Grace

"Tell me a story"
She says this while looking
intently into my face.
"Not from a book" she says, pointing
"from your mouth"
                    From my heart

She tells me where the story is –
The setting
She tells me who is in it –
The characters
and she and I must be in
leading roles
She tells me the problem –
The conflict
otherwise the story is boring

She is a dramatic child,
fully able to reach
the delicious abilities
to feel it all deeply
sorrow and joy
impish mischief
and delighted discovery.

The world is a stage
our mere-ness
is illusion and
certain

Other children join us
join the story
we weave it together
until we get to
                    The End.

and they say *"Again!"*
another story
we,
    as God
            love a good story.

Soul Kin

It happened in Mervyn's once
another woman and I
were pawing through clearance items;
our eyes met and
we recognized each other.

Exchanging words we tried to
establish
the logical possibilities
of our connection –
Baseball? Ballet?
Our children's schools?
Forty-niner games?
Our work place? Our husbands?
Clubs, events, family, hobbies?
We must have spent five minutes
just listing off the touch points;
we never found one
to which we both belonged

Not in this lifetime,
She said, shrugging.
I nodded
We embraced briefly
And each went on our shopping ways

I know this happens to me
Quite often
I recognize you
even though I don't know you
And you recognize me
divinely connected
beyond
what we
can explain
through today's tongue.

On This Side

The void leaps up before me
I am terrified and tempted.

Behind me lies the chaos
of being in the world,

our imperfect bodies
striving toward an unachievable goal.
Perfection does not lie on this side of
birth and death

unknown is at once magnetic
and repellent.

We come to experience the vastness
of our interconnected Love

and then feel the isolation
of not knowing –

uncertainty in how to help
each other,

when we can only
save ourselves.

Being Hope
– To His Holiness

The leaf does not know it is a small part of the whole
Or understand the tree as itself
But the stories of many leaves make up the now, yet and then
And the tree knows the leaf

The shadow cast on the ground is not the object that lies between
Nor the incredible light that is the source of all
But without the shadow we would not define the contrasts
Or see and feel the coolness of less light

The reflection is not the face that its surface makes perceivable
Nor the depth of truth that is behind that face
But the loneliness of self would overwhelm without the otherness of its shine
And in the mirror lies our power to change the world

Your are not the solution to a puzzle
Nor the unspiraling of the great circle
But without the hope your tree shadow reflects
No one would work to reach the beginning

3 a.m. Wednesday May 14, 1997

Fire and Ash

When your volcano erupts
and the spewing anger covers me
up with fire and ash,
my breath is held in hopes
that it will not trigger my own explosion
because, you could kill me
with a word
or a blow
you could
stop the part of me that grows

as you have in the past.

And you say, *sorry*
but you resent it
and really you are pissed and
want me to be
what you want.

Maybe deservedly so.

I only know that stripped to the bone
of the flesh and muscle
of tissue and tendon
I must once again
rebuild myself.

Its not fair, you say,
I know its not
believe me,
I know its not.

Watching Jonah learn to skip

He calls over to me,
this earnest scientist
who, at three years old
finds mystery and humor
Everywhere

"Watch this"
and begins the complicated
mosaic of electrical impulse
Experience
Will
Attention
that moves his organic
hardware through the soup of
gravity and circumstance
with hops and bumps and jumps

He gestures toward his
seemingly independent-thinking knees
with a look of admiration
and joy
illuminating his open face

"Do you want to see that again?"
his impossibly wide
smile re-ignites
my own smile
my own wonder
at the body that carries us
through this existence

Humanity

Our love
is
beyond space
and time
the heat of this
moment
radiates forward and
backward in shadow echoes

The epicenter
is where the true
energy
abounds
let death
be the tool
by which we live
more fully
       Alive
more fully
       Ourselves
insoluble
and
in constant exchange
forever and never
the same

After 20 Minutes of Solo Ecstatic Dancing on my Living Room Floor

I have been given such gifts
words choke in my throat
as I reach,
I stretch, bend and shake
toward expressing
the utter astonishment
the deep wonder
the overpowering gratitude
at this moment
I am
awake

Glimpsing Miracles

My body...........periscope of the gods!
The many eyed,
        billion-feelered,
                trillion-toungued
                        vibrationally-differed,
molecularly one thing.
I
SEE
through –
glimpsing miracles
framed by
the narrow focus of this
        organic evolved
                relationship-dependent
                        structure of
consciousness.

Viewing
these tender sapling
        aspects of me
to my horror
        to my wonder and delight,

I come closer to courage, closer
to the terror of honestly, honestly
                asking
                    for
                        True Dreams –

allowing the power
      that abides in the
            wholeness of Nothing
                  to flow through me.

Instead of turning on the TV
      I read the Tibetan book of the dead
the thrumming beacon is
so often silenced
          by the noise I requested.

Will I surrender
      what was never mine anyway?
This container of mass and space
      spiraling into the next instant
         will spiral out of reach
             disintegrating the
avenue of perception
of the mirror
   of existence
      but existence will remain
         and in its refrain

      I can begin again
         as everything and nothing

Just Now

I just left the dishwasher open,
distracted by a compelling pull,
walked away from
the cupboards yawning open to swallow the clean coffee cups
to write this down:
last year at this time, the eve before my
birthday,
I buzzed my head…
          my students shared lice with me
               my father was dead
                    my marriage was un-doing
Tonight I am leaving a secure, corporate
but lovely job
for lower paying,
maybe-get-by-by-the-skin-of-my-teeth
Soul-serving work
On the brink of
50
Me
I
.

can't wait to see what the next 50 brings

The Edge of Aging

I keep stumbling over
The edge of aging
This wrinkled hand
This creaking hinge
This blank spot
In the file cabinet
That held the treasures
And torments of a life
A story
That is still unfolding
With a few missing
Pieces

But relentless ticking
And the sounding chimes
Of a heedless clock
A blur of seasons
A tremble in the muscles
A veil between causes

My vision softening
As experience sharpens
My silent wonder
My grief in growing
Toward less in body

And ever more in
Changeless   soul

Completeness

I want to eat you up
every drop every sliver and shiver
of skin and bone
every feeling and flash of thought
every pang and wrench, every gleam and gloat
radiantly calling me toward you

I want to hang my heart
on the tops of trees and mountains
gulp up the smells of forest and lake
devour salt tang of sea and the monstrous
power that sleeps and wakes
with such force

I want to merge with
the creatures of scale and feather
and embrace the suchness of
pure being
I am drawn to lean into the green embrace of
the constant furling and unfurling
of the breath of garden and growth
of death's loamy-rich dark welcome
I yearn for the warm tactile orgasmic
connection with the flesh
of consciousness
I hunger for the completeness
in sunset and whirl winds
the satiation of blistered hands
of work accomplished
or the sighs and pause   Gratitudes and grief
of quiet and song grunt groan   lie on the same circle of change
galloping words trying to lasso   the same note in a different
a sensation or sombulant terror or   part of the song that sings
feast of desire   to every ear

Israel and Palestine   10/15/00

The eyes of the world watch you,
hesitating our hurry,
taking a pausing breath,
we wonder…

Will you continue to
use God
as your symbol
to hate and kill?
Will you deny the symbols God has given
others to bridge between earth and spirit?
Will you let the tide of passion
that has tendrils reaching far into the past
pulse you over the edge of hope
and into the abyss of blind fury?

Or, can you stop with us,
take the breath of wonder,
pause for peace to remind you
that we are one in our quest for wholeness?

Individually a flame resides in each heart
waiting for remembrance,
hushed and still, longing to be joined,
joyfully
with the hearts of others
until the radiance exceeds all symbols

Love waits and watches for an invitation.

 **Let it Be**

An ache starts in my joints
and I know new adventures of
this body
are beginning;
a deep sigh as I try to
estimate how much
energy to put toward pain

Distraction, numbness
the weary familiarity
of the weak points
in the frame of my being

Seeking to become
the instrument of the unseen
when the little me gets
out of the way

You have heard them talk about it
The athletes
The artists
The children
The mentally ill

That zone of non-being
when selfhood's
veil lifts,
turns suddenly
to the bigger thing
with no name

The unheard
calls to each,
offers
moments of freedom
release
from this body of pain

only through
complete
surrender

For my mama on her 67ᵗʰ Birthday

My Mama taught me
When I was 5 weeks old, my father was killed in a car accident,
my mama tried not to be sad when she nursed me, so I would not be sad,
my mama taught me:
Today is the day –
to laugh, to learn, to say I love you.
Today is the day.

When I was a small child, my mama gave me gifts of unending love,
Your father is still with you, and you have another father's love as well,
My mama taught me:
Love doesn't end
relationships change, life shifts, energy moves.
Love doesn't end

As I grew, my mama painted, wove, created,
gave me nostalgic memories of linseed oil and turpentine
My mama taught me:
You are given artistic gifts, give them away
don't wait for recognition or to be the best.
Do what you love.

When I struggled, when I was outraged at the world's cruelty,
when I was seeking to be as others,
My mama taught me:
You are a precious gift, just as you are
don't let other's decide that for you.
You are exactly who you should be, right now.

Whenever we went out into the world, or observed creation
in our own backyard or Alaska, or camping,
My mama taught me:
All life is wondrous; all things support each other,
nothing is without meaning or importance.
Revere all living things

When I dreamed, or imagined or fell silent –
when I rebelled, held my ground, or stood up
My mama taught me:
Honor your inner life; it is as important as what happens outside
Your heart knows what your mind cannot fathom.
Follow your heart

When, as a teenager I was disillusioned with the world,
when I judged others, or in fear avoided differences
My mama taught me:
A light resides in each person, no matter how buried
in pain and experience, in anger or hatred
All human beings are innately worthy of love and respect.

When I grew and wanted to make my world better,
when I was overwhelmed with the work needing doing
My mama taught me:
Give of your overflow, not of your essence
be a pebble in a pond, start your kindness here.
Know each thing you do makes a difference

As I had my own children and feared for their well-being,
wanting to protect them, suddenly cautious of every person's intentions
My mama taught me:
Trust life, nurture love, let them grow as they are meant to –
each sorrow carves out space for the next joy.
All life is this package deal

Now as my children are grown, and I strive to be the best me
sometimes discouraged, sometimes jubilant, sometimes peaceful,
My mama taught me:
Those of us, who are less broken, must help those of us who are more so,
each of us has an obligation to let our light shine, and
reflect other's light back to them.
Everything is unfolding as it should

In the great mystery of life, in the hurried pace of our doing,
there is a being-ness that sustains us, and links us,
My mama taught me:
There are no true endings; there are circles and transitions,
there are movements and stillness.

And there is always, always love

About the Author

January Handl is an Early Head Start Home Visitor in her local community. She resides in Boulder Creek with 2 dogs and a cat – she has written poetry since she could write and simply lives in awe of existence.

More books from River Sanctuary Publishing...

Affirmations for Everyday Living: Create more clarity, success and joy in your daily life! by Annie Elizabeth, 2009. $17.95

The Unorthodox Life: Walking Your Own Path to the Divine, by Kathy McCall, 2009. $15.95

Notes to Self: Meditations on Being, by Christy Deena, 2011. $15.95

A Space Between: Adventures and Lessons Between Lives, by Ardeth DeVries, 2010. $15.95

How Alternation Can Change Your Life: Finding the Rhythms of Health and Happiness, by Andrew Oser, 2010. $15.95

American Maze, a novel by Ralph Peduto, 2010. $16.95

Illuminating the Mundane: Transformational Silk Painting and Haiku, (full color) by Billie Furuichi, 2010. $18.95

Available from:

www.spiritualpathfinder.com

River Sanctuary Publishing
P.O. Box 1561
Felton, California 95018
www.riversanctuarypublishing.com

We offer custom book design and production with worldwide availability through print-on-demand, with the best author-friendly terms in the industry. Specializing in inspirational, spiritual and self-help books, biography, and memoirs.

CPSIA information can be obtained at www.ICGtesting.com

232815LV00003B/20/P